Let's Grow
a Garden

Let's Grow
a Garden

ANGELA WILKES

How to use this book

Let's Grow a Garden shows you how to grow flowers, herbs, fruits, and vegetables on windowsills, balconies, and patios. Below are some points to look for on each page when using this book, and a list of things to remember.

Equipment
Illustrated checklists show you which tools to have ready before you start a project.

The things you need
The items to collect for each project are clearly shown to help you check that you have everything you need.

Step-by-step
Step-by-step photographs and clear instructions tell you exactly what to do at each stage of a gardening project.

Things to remember

- Read all the instructions and gather together everything you will need before you begin a project.

- Check when to plant different things and which growing conditions they like best.

- Put on an apron or old shirt and roll up your sleeves before you start.

- Be careful when using sharp scissors. Do not use them unless there is an adult there to help you.

- When you have finished planting things, clean your garden tools, straighten up any mess, and put everything away.

- Water and check your seeds and plants regularly once you have planted them and watch them as they grow.

- Be patient. Do not give up if things do not start to grow right away.

A DK PUBLISHING BOOK

Editor Sarah Johnston
Designers Caroline Potts and Adrienne Hutchinson
DTP Designer Almudena Díaz
Managing Editor Jane Yorke
Managing Art Editor Chris Scollen
US Editor Kristin Ward
Production Ben Smith
Photography Dave King

First American Edition, 1997
2 4 6 8 10 9 7 5 3 1
Published in the United States by DK Publishing, Inc.
95 Madison Avenue, New York, New York 10016
Visit us on the World Wide Web as http://www.dk.com.

Copyright © 1997 Dorling Kindersley Limited, London
Projects originally published in *My First Garden Book*, *My First Nature Book*,
and *My First Green Book* Copyright © 1996, 1994, 1996
Dorling Kindersley Limited, London

A catalog record for this book is available from the Library of Congress.

ISBN 0-7894-1557-7

Color reproduction by Colourscan
Printed and bound in Italy by L.E.G.O.

CONTENTS

PIP PLANTING   6

COLLECTING SEEDS   8

PLANTING SEEDS   10

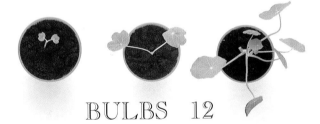

BULBS   12

SPRING FLOWERS   14

A BOTTLE GARDEN   16

WORLD IN A BOTTLE   18

HANGING BASKETS   20

GARDEN IN A BASKET   22

DESERT GARDEN   24

DESERT IN MINIATURE   26

MAKING A WILDLIFE GARDEN   28

WILDLIFE GARDEN   30

PIP PLANTING

Every time you eat fruit, you throw away the pips (small fruit seeds) or pit in the middle, but have you ever thought of planting them instead? If you give the pips the right conditions and are patient, you will be surprised at what will grow: Many pips produce handsome plants. The best time of year to plant pips is in the spring. Here you can find out what to do.

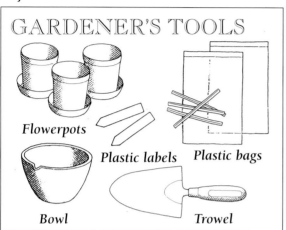

GARDENER'S TOOLS

Flowerpots

Plastic labels   Plastic bags

Bowl   Trowel

Grape pips

Peach pit

Orange or
lemon pips

You will need

Different pips and pits:

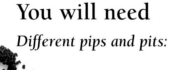

Apple pips

Seeds and
potting soil

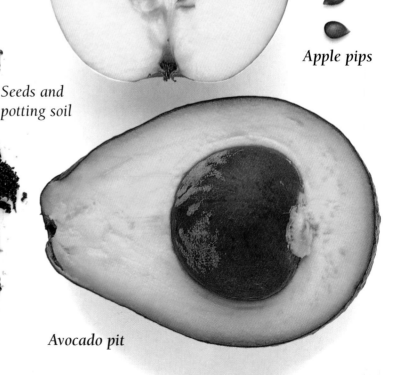

Avocado pit

What to do

1. Soak big pits in water for 24 hours. Put some potting soil in a bowl and water it. Stir it well, then fill small pots with it.

2. Plant avocado pits pointed end up, sticking out of the soil. Plant pips about ½ in (1 cm) down in the pots of soil.

3. Label each pot to say what is in it. Put each pot in a plastic bag and tie the bag at the top, then put the pots in a warm, dark place.

The growing plant

Check the flowerpots every day. As soon as you see a shoot in one of them, move it to a light place and take off the plastic bag. Water the young plant regularly, just enough to keep the soil moist, and watch it grow. Here you can see the first stages in the development of an avocado plant.

New, young leaves

The first leaves soon grow fairly large.

FROM PIT TO PLANT

Avocado pits take six to seven weeks to sprout. The pit splits, a root grows down into the soil, and a shoot emerges at the top.

The stem grows quickly and the first leaves begin to open out.

Young side shoots

If the plant seems to be growing too tall, pinch out the growing shoot at the top. This encourages the plant to grow bushier.

When the plant shows signs of growing too big for its pot, move it to a fresh pot of soil the next size up.

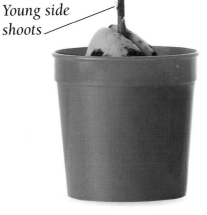

COLLECTING SEEDS

Seeds come in all shapes and sizes. Some are as fine as dust and others look like stones. Some are encased in a juicy fruit; others have their own tiny parachutes. And it isn't just flowers that grow from seeds. Many trees, vegetables, fruits, and grasses do, too. See how many different sorts of seeds you can collect. Below are some to look for.

EQUIPMENT

Scissors

Envelopes

Pencil

Seeds to collect

Acorns (from oak trees)

Maple seeds

Horse chestnuts

Tree seeds

The best time to collect tree seeds is early in the fall, when they have just fallen from the trees. If you wait too long, many seeds will have been taken for food by birds and animals.

Seeds in pinecones

Grass seeds and grains

You may be able to find grains like wheat along the edges of farmland in summer. If not, collect different types of seeds from wild grasses.

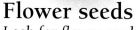

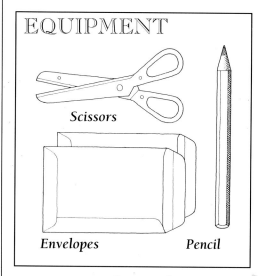

Wild grasses

Wheat

Flower seeds

Look for flower seeds once the petals have died and a seed head has formed. How do you think the seeds are scattered?

Thistledown

Poppy seeds

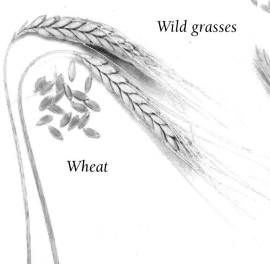

Vegetable seeds

Many kinds of dried beans and peas are seeds. Soak them for 24 hours before planting them.

Runner beans

Black-eyed peas

Adzuki beans

Flageolet beans

Fruit seeds

Cut fruit in half to find the seeds.*
Some types of fruits have seeds and others pits.

Apple seeds

Avocado pit

Lemon seeds

Grape seeds

Harvesting flower seeds

1 Cut a flower when the petals have died. Hold the flower upside down and shake the seeds onto a piece of paper.

2 Fold the piece of paper as shown and pour the flower seeds into a small envelope. Use one envelope for each type of seed.

3 Seal the envelope and label it clearly. Keep it in a dark, dry drawer if you are saving the seeds to plant in the spring.

*Be careful with sharp knives. Ask an adult to help you.

PLANTING SEEDS

If you plant flower seeds indoors in early spring, they will be big enough to plant outside once the weather is warmer. You can grow most *annuals* and *biennials** from seed. Read the backs of seed packets to find out exactly when to plant different flowers, what growing conditions they need, and how often to water them.

You will need

Seeds and potting soil

Ties for plastic bags

Plant labels

Acorns

Nasturtium seeds

Sunflower seeds

Poppy seeds

Plastic bags

What to do

GARDEN TOOLS

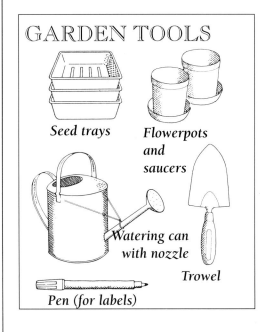

Seed trays

Flowerpots and saucers

Watering can with nozzle

Trowel

Pen (for labels)

1 Fill the flowerpots and seed trays with potting soil to about ½ in (1 cm) down from the top of the pot. Water the soil lightly.

2 Push each big seed about ½ in (1 cm) deep into the soil. Label each pot with the name of the seed you have planted.

Annuals live for one year. Biennials live for two years, but usually only flower the second year.

3 Plant small seeds in seed trays. Sprinkle the seeds onto the potting soil. Cover them with a thin layer of soil. Label the tray.

4 Tie plastic bags over the flowerpots and seed trays and put them in a warm, dark place.** Check the seeds every day.

5 As soon as shoots appear, take off the plastic bags and move the seeds into the light. Water the soil enough to keep it damp.

**Such as a cupboard.

FROM SEED TO PLANT

Nasturtiums are among the easiest flowers to grow. Here you can see how a seedling develops. This plant stayed in one pot, but seedlings planted in seed trays will need to be carefully dug up and moved to separate pots, or into the garden, once they are big enough.

You can just see the nasturtium's first two leaves.

The seedling grows fast. The first two leaves grow bigger. The stem shoots up between them and more leaves appear. The young plant needs a lot of light.

Buds appear, then the nasturtium starts to flower. Since it is a climbing plant, you should tie it to a garden stake as it grows bigger. The plant will twine around the stake.

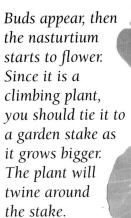

BULBS

Many of the prettiest spring flowers grow from bulbs and are easy to grow indoors. Buy bulbs in the fall and plant them right away, to flower the following spring. Grow only the same plants in any one pot, so that they all flower at the same time. Bulbs have to be kept in a cold, dark place, so they can form strong roots which will help them bloom well later. Turn the page to see a stunning array of flowers grown from bulbs.

Gravel or clay pellets

You will need

Different bulbs:

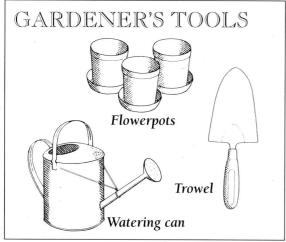

GARDENER'S TOOLS

Flowerpots

Trowel

Watering can

Hyacinths

Dwarf tulips

Daffodils

Planting bulbs

1 Shovel a little gravel or some clay pellets into the bottom of your flowerpots or containers to prevent the soil from getting soggy.

2 Half fill the flowerpots with potting soil. Instead of the potting soil you could use special bulb fiber if you like.

3 Arrange big bulbs close together with their pointed ends up. Add more soil. Let the ends poke out of the soil.

Potting soil

What is a bulb?
Here the bulb of a hyacinth in flower has been cut in half, so that you can see what is inside it.

Grape hyacinths _Crocuses_

Daffodils

Miniature irises

Food supply
A bulb is like an onion inside. It is a kind of underground food store. The plant rests for most of the year, then uses the food in the bulb to grow.

Roots
Bulbs have to grow strong roots before they can be brought into the light.

4 Arrange small bulbs with the pointed ends up. Add enough soil to cover them and fill the pot to 1 in (2 cm) below the rim.

5 Water the pots, then put them in a cold, dark place for 8 to 12 weeks. Check the soil occasionally, to make sure it is moist.

SPRING FLOWERS

When the bulbs have shoots about 1 in (2 cm) tall, move the flowerpots into the light, but keep them in a cool place. Most bulbs will flower three to five months after planting. They will flower best in a cool room. When the flowers have died, cut off the dead flower heads and let the leaves dry up, then plant the bulbs outside if you can, since they will not flower indoors again. The beautifully colored flowers shown here all bloom in early spring.

DWARF DAFFODIL

"Tête-à-tête" is a tiny golden daffodil with swept-back petals.

CHIONODOXA

Commonly known as "Glory-of-the-snow," it has starry blue flowers with white eyes.

CROCUS

*One of the first spring flowers, it has funnel-shaped white, purple, or yellow flowers. Grows from a corm.**

SCILLA

This tiny plant has small, bright blue, bell-shaped flowers.

A stem that grows under the surface of the soil.

PUSCHKINIA
This tiny rock garden plant has spikes of star-shaped white or blue flowers.

HYACINTH
Hyacinths have heavy spikes of sweetly scented flowers, which may need supporting with garden stakes. Try growing hyacinths in water in special jars so that you can watch the roots grow.

WATER LILY TULIP
A dwarf tulip that has white flowers with red and yellow centers. Like other lily-flowered tulips, the flowers open out flat in the sun.

15

A BOTTLE GARDEN

You can create a mossy garden in your home by growing things in a bottle. Bottle gardens keep in a lot of moisture and are good for plants that like to grow in damp places. Any sort of big bottle will do, as long as it has a wide neck. Look for mosses, ferns, and lichens in shady woodlands. Here you can see how to plant them and on the next page is the finished garden.

EQUIPMENT

Pitcher of water

Big spoon

You will need

Different types of mosses

Small pebbles or gravel

A big glass bottle

Peat-based potting soil

Making the garden

1 Spoon a layer of pebbles or gravel into the bottom of the bottle. Add a thin layer of charcoal to keep the soil sweet.

2 Cover the pebbles and charcoal with a deep layer of potting soil. Press the soil down firmly with the spoon.

3 Dig a small hole for the first plant, using the spoon. Gently pick up the plant, as shown, and lower it into the bottle.

4 Cover the plant's roots with soil, then press the soil down firmly all around the plant, using the spoon.

5 Dig a shallow hollow for a clump of moss. Lay the moss in the hollow and gently press down the soil around it.

6 Plant everything in this way, arranging it as prettily as you can. Then carefully pour about a cup of water into the bottle.

Small ferns

Pieces of charcoal

Lichen-covered twigs or bark

17

WORLD IN A BOTTLE

Mosses and ferns are happiest in damp, shady places, so put the bottle garden in a cool place where the light is good, but not bright. It is best to avoid direct sunlight. Once you have made the garden, it should need very little care. You can see what to do on the opposite page. Watch the mosses and ferns to see how they grow or change. In spring, the mosses may grow tiny grasslike stems with capsules on them. These capsules contain the mosses' spores, which are like seeds. You can see three different types of moss with spore capsules at the bottom of the bottle garden here. Ferns also produce spore capsules. They are usually on the undersides of the leaves.

Small fern

Twig covered with lichens. Although mosses and lichens look alike, they are not related. Lichens are a special type of fungus.

Moss with spore capsules

EQUIPMENT

Scissors

Spray bottle

18

Maidenhair fern

Potting soil

Moss with spore capsules

Moss

Watering the garden

Your bottle garden will need very little watering. Just spray it with water occasionally to keep the soil moist.

Pruning

Keep an eye on the condition of your plants. Snip off any dead leaves or pieces of fern with a small pair of scissors.

Open or closed?

Leave the bottle open until there are no drops of water left on the inside of the glass. Then you can put the lid on.

HANGING BASKETS

A hanging basket is one of the prettiest mini-gardens you can make and you can hang it anywhere you want. We used spring flowers in blues and yellows for our basket. For a summer basket, look for fuchsias, geraniums, impatiens, and lobelia. Turn the page for the finished basket.

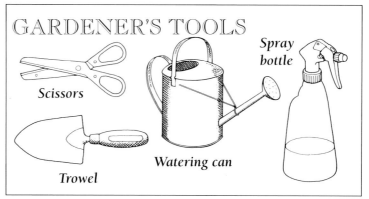

GARDENER'S TOOLS

Scissors

Spray bottle

Trowel

Watering can

You will need

Lightweight potting soil

Pansies

A wire basket with a chain handle

Grape hyacinths

Sphagnum moss

Plastic garbage bag

Primroses

Drumstick primrose

Trailing variegated ivy plants

Planting the basket

1 Line the inside of the wire basket with a thickish layer of sphagnum moss. You should not be able to see any light through it.

2 Cut a piece of plastic bag big enough to line the inside of the basket. Lay it over the moss and trim off any edges that show.

3 Wrap each ivy plant in a small piece of plastic shaped into a cone. The narrow end of the cone should be around the leaves.

Garden In A Basket

Here is the finished basket, overflowing with spring flowers. A hanging basket is very heavy when full, so ask an adult to hang it up for you and check that it is fastened securely. Hang it in a place where you can see the plants fully and make sure that it is low enough for you to water easily.

Planting the basket (continued)

4 Make holes in the plastic liner. Thread the cone-wrapped leaves of the ivy plants through the holes. Pull the plastic cones away.

5 Thread a few more plants through the base of the basket in the same way, then half fill the basket with potting soil.

GRAPE HYACINTHS
These pretty spring flowers grow from bulbs.

SPHAGNUM MOSS

Chain

PRIMROSE

DRUMSTICK PRIMROSE

There are many different sorts of primrose. Most flower in spring.

PANSIES

In mild-weather areas, winter-flowering pansies will flower throughout the winter and spring as long as you deadhead them regularly.

VARIEGATED IVY

Trailing ivy plants are useful for hanging baskets because they provide greenery and trail prettily around the bottom of the basket.

6 Arrange and plant the rest of the plants in the basket. Fill the gaps between the plants with soil and water them well.

Watering

Water and spray the basket just enough to keep the soil damp. Baskets need watering once or twice a day in hot weather.

Deadheading

The plants in the basket will last longer if you regularly snip off any dead flower heads or leaves. Replace any plants that die.

23

DESERT GARDEN

Buy some small succulents to create a miniature desert in your own home. Succulents are plants that can survive without much water since they store it in their fleshy leaves or stems. Choose non-prickly plants with contrasting shapes, colors, and textures and try out different arrangements in a shallow container or tray. Turn the page to see a finished desert garden.

You will need

Small succulents:

Sedum sieboldii

*Wart plant
(Haworthia attenuata)*

GARDENER'S TOOLS

Small spoon

Trowel

Scissors

*Watering
can*

*Gravel or coarse
pebbles*

Potting soil

Coarse sand

*Shallow container
or deep tray*

Hen and chicks (Echeveria)

What to do

1 Put a thin layer of gravel in the bottom of the container. Cover with potting soil until the container is half full.

2 Keeping the plants in their pots, try out different arrangements to see where you want to plant them.

Flaming Katy (Kalanchoe blossfeldiana)

3 Carefully remove the plants from their pots, one at a time, and plant them. Fill in the gaps between them with more soil.

4 Gently spoon coarse sand over the surface of the soil, then water lightly to settle the soil and plants.

Jade plant (Crassula ovata)

Elephant bush (Portulacaria afra)

*Sedum**

*Sedum**

*There are more than 200 different types of sedum.

Desert In Miniature

Succulents like a lot of light, so put the finished mini-desert in a brightly lit window. The plants have a rest period in winter, so water the garden less often then. It is a good idea to put the desert garden outside in a bright, sheltered spot during the warm summer months, since this helps the plants to grow stronger.

Watering

Water the desert garden only when the surface of the soil has dried out. Desert plants like to dry out between waterings.

Trimming

If any of the plants grow "branches" that are long and straggly, cut them off with a small pair of scissors.

ELEPHANT BUSH
(Portulacaria afra)

SEDUM

SEDUM

WART PLANT
(Haworthia attenuata)

FLAMING KATY
This plant's bright flowers last a long time. Replace it when it has stopped flowering, since it won't flower again.

26

The finished garden

The miniature desert garden looks surprisingly green and fresh. To add interest to the garden, you could arrange decorative pebbles or shells around the plants.

JADE PLANT

(Crassula ovata)

This plant is also sometimes known as the money plant.

Replacing plants

1 If a plant grows too big, gently dig it up with a teaspoon and replant it in a flowerpot or container of its own.

HEN AND CHICKS

(Echeveria)

The name comes from this plant's habit of growing baby plants around the main plant.

SEDUM SIEBOLDII

2 Replace the big plant with a smaller one. Slide the new plant out of its pot, plant it, and press the soil and sand around it.

27

MAKING A WILDLIFE GARDEN

One of the best ways to help wildlife flourish close to your home is to create a special garden. You don't need much space. A window box or a large pot will do. Plant the garden with nectar-rich flowers and it will attract butterflies and bees. Here you can see how to plant a window box with late summer flowers.

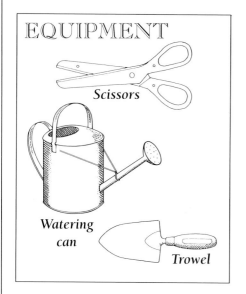

EQUIPMENT

Scissors

Watering can

Trowel

You will need

Heather

A window box or large flowerpot with drainage holes in the bottom

Gravel or clay pellets

Potting soil

What to do

*Marjoram
(or thyme)*

1 Fill the bottom of the window box with a layer of gravel or pellets about 1½ in (3 cm) deep. This lets excess water drain out.

2 With the trowel, put potting soil into the window box, on top of the gravel. The window box needs to be half full.

*Sedum
(Stonecrop)*

3 Keeping the plants in their pots, decide how to arrange them. Tall plants should go at the back and trailing ones at the front.

4 Gently take the first plant out of its pot and put it in the window box. Press it slightly into the soil.

*Chrysanthemums
and Asters*

5 Do the same with the other plants. Fill potting soil in around the plants. Press it down firmly, then water it well.

WILDLIFE GARDEN

And here is the finished window box, full of flowers that will last through late summer. Put the window box on a sunny window ledge, making sure that it is stable and cannot fall. Even if you live in the heart of a city, you will be able to watch the bees and butterflies come in search of nectar.

DAISY HEADS

Moist daisylike flowers are popular with butterflies and bees. In late summer, these creatures flock to chrysanthemums, asters, and sunflowers.

SWEET MARJORAM

The pink flowers of this strongly scented herb attract both bees and butterflies. Another herb that you could use is thyme, which also has small, pretty flowers.

Watering

Water the window box often enough to keep the soil moist. It will need watering every day during warm weather.

STONECROP *(Sedum spectabile)*

A garden plant famous for attracting butterflies, stonecrop has wide heads of tightly packed tiny pink flowers in late summer. It flowers year after year.

HEATHER

This small evergreen shrub produces spikes of pink or purple bell-shaped flowers from midsummer to late fall. It is very popular with bees.

WINDOW BOX

This window box is made of terracotta (clay), rather than plastic. Terracotta absorbs a lot of moisture, so terracotta window boxes and flowerpots need watering more often than plastic ones.

Deadheading

The plants in the window box will continue flowering longer if you regularly pick or snip off any dead flower heads.